GOING FOR IT!

A GYM BAG COMPANION FOR LIVING OUR DREAMS

Thanks for the kind words guys...

"Thank you for publishing Going For It! It has been an inspiration to all the athletes at the Cincinnati Gymnastics Academy; training team through elite. Going For It! is one of my key resources in our sports psychology class. We are ready for Going For It! II."

            - **Mary Lee Tracy**
               USAG Coach of the Year
               Cincinnati Gymnasts Academy, OH

"I have read and re-read Going For It! many times. It has been a valuable source of information for both my gymnasts and myself. Truly an inspiration."

            - **Kelli Hill**
               National Team Coach
               Hill's Angels, MD.

"Going For It! has been a great source of the motivational cues we want our athletes to think about in practice and in competition. Our gymnasts will definitely be carrying Going For It! in their gym bags at the world championships."

            - **Tom and Lori Forster**
               National Team Coaches
               Colorado Aerials. CO.

"Finally! A motivational book for young athletes! This is a 'must read' for all gymnasts and coaches. This book contains positive ideas that gymnasts should use in their daily workouts that will motivate them to reach their dreams. I can't wait to share this book with all the gymnasts and coaches I know."

            - **Steve Elliott**
               Director: Woodward Gymnastics Camp
               Eight Time World Tumbling Champion
               National Team Staff Member

"Going For It! is a must for any athlete who has ever set a goal or dreamed of greatness. Mark has taken the positive motivation techniques of sports psychologists and relayed them in a humorous manner that any gymnast will understand and enjoy."

> **- Tony Gehman**
> President of the Elite Coaches Association
> National Team Coach
> North Stars Gymnastics, NJ.

"I feel that Going For It! is a terrific piece of work. Mark has taken the sound principals of sport psychology and mental training and put them in a readable, thoughtful, and fun format that athletes, coaches and parents are going to find most beneficial."

> **- Dr. Joe Massimo**
> Sports Psychologist
> Member of US Olympic Committee
> Sport Psychology Register

"Mark Gibson's book is filled with wisdom and inspiration. It reminds us of what we can, should and must do to be a success at anything."

> **- Fred Turoff**
> Men's Coach, Temple University

"This book will help all young gymnasts achieve their goals. Not only in gymnastics, but also in life. Every chapter in this book teaches us important lessons about being better people as well as better athletes. I thoroughly enjoyed reading this book."

> **- Constantin Petrescu**
> Former Rumanian Olympic Team Member
> Director - Camp International, Pennsylvania

"Mark has created a world of knowledge for the young athlete. This book will produce many positive learning experiences for them."

> **- Brian Babcock**
> Former National Champion

Going For It!
A Gym Bag Companion For Living Our Dreams

Copyright © 1994 by Mark Gibson

Published by Wind Dancer Publications

United States publication: April 1995

ISBN O-9644172-9-4
Second Printing February 1996
Third Printing July 1996

Wind Dancer Publications
P.O. Box 263 Perkasie, PA 18944
Call 215 257-4584

**If one advances confidently in the
direction of ones dreams and endeavors
to live the life he has imagined,
he will meet with success unexpected
in common hours.**

- Henry David Thoreau

We must teach our athletes to dream

We must teach our athletes that dreams provide us a sense of direction
and the inner strength to persevere when those all around us are quitting.

We must teach our athletes that life does not provide guarantees, just opportunities...
and those who develop the faith to act on the belief that they can succeed will always
finish ahead of those who wait until they know they can succeed.

We must teach our athletes that every dream comes with a price, and they may only
realize the dreams for which they are willing to pay in advance, and pay in full.

We must teach our athletes that dreams are just a destination.
The type of people we become as we journey to our dreams is far more important
than the reward we receive at the end of our journey.

We must teach our athletes that to master gymnastics is to master balance.
When we lose our balance, we fall.
Life works the same way.

Wind Dancer Publications © 1996
Dedicated to the champion in every athlete

For more information about Wind Dancer motivational products please write to:
Wind Dancer Publications P.O. Box 263 Perkasie, PA 18944

This book is dedicated to Donna,
my loving travel companion along
the bumpy dream highway.

Going For It!

"Going for It!"
"Going for What?"
"It."
"what?"
"It."
"What's it?"
"It's it."
"It's what?"
"It."
"What?"
"Forget it."
"Forget what?"

Do you know what your "it" is?
And if you do, do you know how to get "it"?

There is an old song with a line that goes, "You got to have a dream, if you don't have a dream, how you gonna make a dream come true?" What's your dream? Do you want to make it to regionals, the national team, the Olympic team?

Dreams are essential; but simply having a dream is not enough. You must also have a plan of action to make the dream come true. As you put your plan to work you must be able to recognize and deal with things that may distract you from achieving your dream.

That's why I wrote "Going For It!" This book will help you find your dream, embrace your dream, create a plan of action for your dream and then...**GO FOR IT!**

CONTENTS

CONTENTS (continued)

How to read this book

Please read this book thoroughly. I have written it in such a way that you should be able to read the whole thing in about two hours or less. Of course you don't have to read it from cover to cover in one sitting if you don't want to. Every chapter can be read in less than 20 minutes, so if you just want to get through a chapter a day, that's fine with me. I only have one rule, and this is it:

Don't read this book just once.
It was meant to be read over and over.

As you read, keep a handful of colored pens close by. You can use these to highlight key phrases and meaningful passages. Make notes in all the blank spaces and scribble down any ideas that pop into your head as you read. Fill this book up with your ideas and feelings. Write down your dreams, your goals, your fears... anything!

Don't just read with your eyes...
Read with your whole mind.

And when you are done reading...

START DOING!!!

CHAPTER 1

HABITS

FRIEND OR FOE

DRAGGING ANCHORS

BECOMING AN EXPERT

REPETITION VS. CORRECTION

BUILDING THE YOU, YOU WANT TO BE

TRADE YOUR ANCHORS FOR WINGS

MASTER YOUR HABITS

OR

THEY WILL

MASTER YOU

FRIEND OR FOE?

*One definition of insanity is to do the same thing
over and over and expect a different result.*

Jimmy habitually keeps good form on his cast to handstand. Good for him, that is one skill he no longer has to think about. Countless perfect repetitions have developed Jimmy's strength and coordination to the point where keeping form on a cast to handstand is easy.

Sadly, at the other end of the gym, Jenny is still casting to a handstand with bent, straddled legs. That bad habit is just one small burden holding Jenny back from achieving her dreams.

Always remember, developing good habits will put you on the fast track to your dreams. Unfortunately, developing bad habits is a trip down a one way street to frustration.

I control my habits. My habits do not control me.

TRYING TO

REACH YOUR GOALS

WITHOUT FIRST

CHANGING

YOUR BAD HABITS

IS LIKE TRYING TO SWIM

WITH A

50 LB. ANCHOR

DRAGGING ANCHORS

*The key to success is to learn to do something right
and then do it right every time.*
-Pat Riley

You have a choice of two ways to learn a new skill. Which would you choose?

> **With state of the art equipment, huge pits, plenty of landing mats and the best instruction.**

Or...

> **With 50 year old equipment, no pits, no landing mats and no instruction.**

Did you choose the first answer? If so, why? Did you think that the second choice would be too hard? If your answer to that last question is yes, then let me ask you one more question.

If you prefer not to learn things the hard way, why are you trying to learn twists on floor with a slow back handspring, or a giant on bars with a big back arch?

Trying to learn the big skills with poorly developed basics is the hardest way to learn anything. And yet every day in every gym there are hard working, frustrated gymnasts failing to learn new skills. They are talented enough to learn the new skills but their old bad habits are holding them back.

I refuse to be held back from achieving my full potential by old bad habits.

WHATEVER

YOU PRACTICE

MOST

YOU WILL

BECOME

AN EXPERT AT

BECOMING AN EXPERT

*Every time you let yourself practice a movement incorrectly,
you are increasing your ability to do it wrong.*
-Dan Millman

If Cathy practices a piked front handspring vault for five years, guess what? At the end of those five years she will be an expert at performing piked front handsprings.

Ask yourself these questions:

**What habits (good or bad) do I reinforce at every workout that
will add up to define the kind of gymnast I will be in five years?**

**When people talk about my gymnastics do I want them to say,
"she/he is a great looking gymnast," or, do I want them to say,
"look, that's the result of a lifetime of sloppy workouts."?**

Whether you become an expert at good gymnastics or an expert at bad gymnastics will depend on one simple decision you can make today. This is it:

**DECIDE WHAT YOU WOULD LIKE TO BE AN EXPERT AT AND THEN
COMMIT YOURSELF TO PRACTICING ONLY THOSE THINGS THAT
WILL HELP YOU ACHIEVE EXCELLENCE.**

What I demand from myself is a reflection of how much faith I have in myself.
I therefore demand nothing less than my personal best.

PRACTICE

DOES NOT

MAKE PERFECT...

PERFECT PRACTICE

MAKES PERFECT

REPETITION VS. CORRECTION

Man cannot win by focusing on winning.
Winning is the result of doing many small things correctly.
-John Wooden

Hard work will always guarantee results. Unfortunately, they may not be the results we were looking for. If we come into the gym every day and practice bad gymnastics we will definitely get better at... say it with me... **BAD GYMNASTICS!**

You may want to get the following tattooed back to front on your forehead so you can see it every time you look into a mirror.

GREAT GYMNASTICS
IS NOT THE RESULT
OF A MILLION
REPETITIONS

GREAT GYMNASTICS
IS THE RESULT
OF A MILLION
CORRECTIONS

Go ahead. Rush to the tattoo parlor right now. **It's that important!**

I know that it's not how many times I do a thing that counts. It's how many times I do it right!

THE KIND OF GYMNAST

YOU ARE TODAY

IS THE RESULT

OF HOW YOU TRAINED YESTERDAY

****

THE KIND OF GYMNAST

YOU WILL BE TOMORROW

WILL BE THE RESULT

OF HOW YOU TRAIN TODAY

BUILDING THE YOU, YOU WANT TO BE

Working hard becomes a habit, a serious kind of fun.
-Mary Lou Retton

Every workout is one small step towards the kind of gymnast you are destined to become in ten years or so.

Try this little exercise:

Ask any current or former gymnast (not your coach) who is over the age of 20, how they would train differently if they had a second chance. As you listen to their answer, remind yourself of this universal truth:

THERE ARE NO SECOND CHANCES!

That's right, there are no second chances! This is not a trial run. This is the real thing. You have one shot and one shot only to make it as a gymnast. You cannot come back at age 25 and try again.

AT EVERY WORKOUT YOU ARE EITHER BUILDING
FUTURE DREAMS OR FUTURE DISAPPOINTMENTS

I have less than 10 years to make my gymnastic dreams come true.
I never waste a single workout.

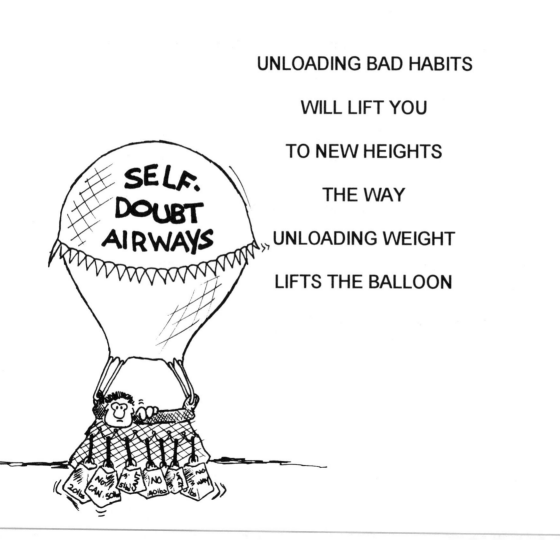

UNLOADING BAD HABITS

WILL LIFT YOU

TO NEW HEIGHTS

THE WAY

UNLOADING WEIGHT

LIFTS THE BALLOON

TRADE YOUR ANCHORS FOR WINGS

Get into the habit of training like a champion.
-M.G.

Remember these six essential steps for turning your bad habits into good ones.

1. **RECOGNIZE** the bad habit (you can't fix it if you don't know you have it.)

2. **REFUSE** to accept the bad habit as a part of you or your future workouts.

3. **REPLACE** the bad habit with a good one.

4. **REPAIR** the damage caused by the old habit by practicing the new one exclusively.

5. **REEVALUATE** the progress of the new habit on a regular basis.

6. **REAP THE REWARDS.** You must take a great deal of pride in the development of your new habit and become comfortable with the new behavior, accepting it as a part of your identity. If you don't take these steps you may find yourself slipping back into the easy comfort of your old familiar bad habits.

Today I will list all my bad habits and then use these six steps
to free myself of their negative influence.

WHAT THIS CHAPTER MEANS TO ME

The three habits I am most proud of are: **The three habits I am most committed to changing are:**

1.   1.

2.   2.

3.   3.

The three phrases my coach has to repeat to me over and over are:

1.

2.

3.
My coach repeats these phrases so often because **I have not committed myself to improving my performance in these areas.**

I have asked three older gymnasts how they would train if they could be my age again.
They told me:

1._____
    Gymnast's name

2._____
    Gymnast's name

3._____
    Gymnast's name

THE LAST WORD

Think of your gymnastics like a ladder. A ladder that leads to your dreams. At every workout you either take a step up the ladder closer to your dreams, or you take a step down the ladder away from your dreams.

Unfortunately you do not get to stay on this ladder as long as you want. One day (when you retire from competition) you will have to leave the ladder. If, at this point, you have been climbing at 90% of your workouts, you will probably have reached your dreams. Congratulations!

On the other hand, if you spent only 50% of your workouts climbing up the ladder, you will almost certainly not have reached your dreams. What a shame!

Every day you walk into your gym is another golden opportunity for you to develop the winning habits of a champion. Every turn up on the apparatus can bring you one small step closer to your dreams.

ONE PERSON'S
FEAR
IS ANOTHER'S
EXCITEMENT

CHAPTER 2

FEAR

FACE UP TO FEAR

FEAR IS A TEST

FEAR AND OPPORTUNITY

FEAR AND DESIRE

FEAR IS FUN

FEAR IS A DOOR, NOT A BARRIER

"CAUTION"- THINKING AHEAD

The world is not divided into...

GROUPS OF PEOPLE

WHO HAVE FEARS

AND

PEOPLE WHO DO NOT

It is divided into ...

GROUPS OF PEOPLE

WHO GO AFTER THEIR DREAMS

DESPITE THEIR FEARS

AND

PEOPLE WHO DO NOT

FACE UP TO FEAR

He who is not courageous enough to take risks
will accomplish nothing in life.
-Muhammad Ali

We are not given a choice of whether or not we will have fears (everybody has them). We are, however, given a choice of how we would like to respond to our fears.

When faced with fear we can choose to...

Formulate a plan to overcome the fear.

Or...

Allow the fear to overcome us

If we choose to deal with fear by creating a plan of action to overcome it, we will keep ourselves on track to our dreams.

However, if we choose to give in to our fear we allow our dreams to slip away.

Starting from today, why not decide to respond to your fears in a manner that will move you towards your dreams instead of away from them?

I do not try to ignore my fears and I know I can't chase them away.
I accept my fears as a part of who I am and I deal with them.

FEAR IS

NATURE'S WAY

OF TESTING YOU

TO SEE

IF YOU

ARE SERIOUS

ABOUT YOUR GOALS

FEAR IS A TEST

Don't be frightened if things seem difficult in the beginning.
That is only the initial impression.
-Olga Korbut

You set your goals, you work hard, and just when everything seems to be going great, **WHAM!** Your hand slips on vault and there you are, sitting on the mat, shaking like a leaf, and wondering if hanging out at the mall wouldn't be such a bad thing.

Consider these questions...

Does fear just make me more determined to perform better?

Or...

Does fear just make me wish there was an easier way to achieve my goals?

To become a true champion we must accept the fact that there is no easy path to excellence. We have to expect frequent tests as we pursue our goals. After all, the world can only handle so many champions. Fear is an excellent tool for separating those who are serious about their goals from those who are not fully committed.

I recognize fear as a test of my commitment. I pass with honors.

WHERE THERE IS FEAR

THERE IS OPPORTUNITY

****

WHERE THERE IS OPPORTUNITY

THERE IS FEAR

FEAR AND OPPORTUNITY

You should feel nervous! Your body is preparing for a unique demand.
-Dan Millman

There is only one way to eliminate all fear...

DO NOTHING!

That's right, do absolutely nothing! Never have dreams or goals. Never learn new skills or new routines. Definitely do not enter meets; for that matter, don't even come to workout. To really play it safe stay in bed all day and try to sleep most of the time.

Do you think you could live like this? Some people do. And are they free from fear? Actually the opposite is true. These people are fears greatest prisoners. In all honesty there is no way you can avoid fear. The best you can hope for is to eliminate the grip fear has on your dreams. One of the best ways to do this is to look at fear from a different angle.

Instead of focusing on the fear that comes with every opportunity,
why not, instead, focus on the opportunity that comes with every fear.

The precious gift of opportunity often comes wrapped as an ugly package of fear. Never make the mistake of throwing out the gift because you didn't like the way it came wrapped.

I have learned that the most important things in life are usually the hardest to accomplish.

PEAK MOMENTS

USUALLY HAPPEN

JUST SECONDS AFTER

WE DEFEAT A FEAR

THAT WAS

HOLDING US BACK

FROM A DESIRE

FEAR AND DESIRE

Fear and desire are opposite sides of the same coin.
-Denis Waitley

It's Jenna's first double back tuck on floor without a spot. Her belly is in knots, her palms are sweating and her heart feels like it may just pound right out of her chest. Yes, she is very nervous, but she knows that she is ready. So, she takes a deep breath and **"GOES FOR IT!"**

As her feet land safely on the mat again, how do you think she feels?

- Triumphant?
- Thrilled?
- Happy?
- Confident?
- Superhuman?

The correct response of course is... all of the above.

Life's two greatest motivators are fear and desire. You either fear something so much that you are motivated to let go of a desire, or , you desire something so much that you are motivated to overcome your fear to achieve your desire. Everything we do comes with elements of both fear and desire. We can't change that, but we can change the ratios. Always ask yourself. "Am I being motivated more by my fears or my desires?"

I stay focused on my desires. I deal with my fears.

ONE GYMNAST'S

FEAR

IS ANOTHER'S

EXCITEMENT

FEAR IS FUN

Fear is probably the thing that limits performance more than anything.
-Mark Allen

I am not kidding. Fear can be a lot of fun...

WHEN YOU ARE
CONFIDENT IN YOUR ABILITY
TO HANDLE THE FEAR.

Have you used your past encounters with fear as a means to develop your self-confidence to a point where you now get excited by the opportunity to challenge new fears?

Believe it or not, there are a lot of people out there who really do think this way. From their own experience they have discovered that taking on their fears and defeating them is a great feeling. They are smart enough to know that defeating fear is not always a case of just, "going for it." Sometimes conquering a fear can take months or even years. Fear crushing is often a lengthy process involving a carefully thought out plan of action.

Sometimes these people are mistakenly called "fearless." They, on the other hand, know that nothing could be further from the truth. They have fears just like anybody else. The difference is, **they have made the simple decision to grow stronger from their encounters with fear.**

What some people call being fearless I call being prepared.

NEVER LET

YOUR FEARS

STAND IN THE WAY

OF YOUR

DREAMS

FEAR IS A DOOR, NOT A BARRIER

Feel the fear and do it anyway.
-Susan Jeffers

Imagine yourself walking through a network of long corridors past rows and rows of doors. Behind every door is a hidden world of exciting opportunity.

One long corridor happens to be the gymnastics corridor. Along its length are the Yurchenko door, the double tuck door, the reverse hecht door and many more. Unfortunately, not every door will be unlocked to you. The only way to find out is to push each door and then step through the open ones.

Fear of the unknown prevents most gymnasts from trying all the doors of opportunity. Oh, they may give the handle a little jiggle, but they don't lean into the doors and shove them with all their weight.

**Fear of the unknown does not have to be a barrier,
and it is never a reason to give up on a dream.**

In fact, quite the opposite is true. Fear lets you know that you are still pushing open new doors along the corridor of your dreams and stepping into unfamiliar and therefore uncomfortable territory.

Butterflies in my belly remind me that I am trying unfamiliar things
and thus growing, both as a person and a gymnast.

IGNORING FEAR IS LIKE

RACING A SPORTS

CAR TO YOUR DREAMS;

SPEEDING THROUGH

ALL THE TRAFFIC LIGHTS

WITHOUT EVER SLOWING DOWN.

NINE TIMES OUT OF TEN

YOU WILL GET LUCKY.

BUT THAT TENTH TIME....

"CAUTION"- THINKING AHEAD

I work on a certain move constantly, then, finally, it doesn't seem so risky to me.
The move stays dangerous and looks dangerous to my foes, but not to me.
Hard work has made it easy. That's my secret. That's why I win.
-Nadia Comaneci

As we already discussed, just "chucking" a skill is not always the smartest way to deal with your fears. Fear is often an opportunity for us to slow down and think about what we are doing. Maybe we need to consider a different skill or a new progression. Is there a possibility that we don't fully understand the skill yet?

The next time you feel fear, consider these questions:

Am I fully prepared, both mentally and physically to perform this skill or handle this situation?

Have I carefully thought through all the possible consequences?

Is my mind focused on my performance or on what could go wrong?

Fear is never a stop sign. A warning sign perhaps, maybe a detour, but always an opportunity to think and ask, **is this the best way for me?**

Fear makes me think about different ways to achieve my goals.
Fear never makes me think about quitting.

WHAT THIS CHAPTER MEANS TO ME

Three things that used to scare me, but don't anymore are:
1.

2.

3.
I overcame those fears by:

Three things that presently scare me most are:
1.

2.

3.
I will develop a plan of action to overcome these fears. I will pass this test of my commitment.

To overcome these fears I will break them down into small steps that I can handle.
The first step for each of the three fears listed above is:
1.

2.

3.

Once I have conquered these steps I will keep moving forward by taking the next steps, followed by the next, followed by the next....

THE LAST WORD

If the only people who ever achieved their dreams were those who had no fear, then we could all agree that fear is the reason we don't achieve our dreams. But, this is not the case. As we have established, everybody has fears.

So, if everybody has fears and yet there are so many people out there making their dreams come true despite their fears, then we must also agree that fear is not the problem.

The problem is how we choose to deal with fear. If we accept fear as an inevitable part of going after our dreams, we will gradually develop the confidence to handle our fears.

When you choose to be the master of your fears, fears cease to be barriers. Instead they become useful road signs along the dream highway. They will point you in the safest direction and warn you of upcoming hazards.

Responding to your fears wisely will keep you in the fast lane... furthest from the exits.

YOU CAN HAVE ANYTHING
YOU WANT...
BUT YOU CAN'T HAVE EVERYTHING

CHAPTER 3

GOALS
3, 2, 1, LIFT OFF!

THE RULES

LONG RANGE GOALS

MEDIUM AND SHORT RANGE GOALS

TODAY GOALS

OUTCOME GOALS

THE PROBLEM WITH OUTCOME GOALS

PERFORMANCE GOALS

SETTING PERFORMANCE GOALS

NO ONE HAS EVER

ACHIEVED THEIR DREAMS

BY JUST DREAMING

***

TO MAKE YOUR DREAMS COME TRUE

YOU MUST COMBINE DREAMING

WITH DOING

3, 2, 1, LIFT OFF

*We all have dreams. But, in order to make dreams into reality it takes
an awful lot of determination, dedication, self-discipline and effort.*
-Jesse Owens

Dreams are the rocket fuel that can blast us to the stars. Unfortunately, our dreams, like rockets, will sit on the launch pad forever if their fuel is not ignited. To make our dreams take off into the world of reality we must ignite them with action.

Ask yourself this question:

Do I arrive at every workout with goals of what I intend to do that day?

Or:

Do I just drift into the gym dreaming about the day I'll go to nationals?

Without goals your dreams will forever remain just dreams.

Remember this:

**WHILE THE DREAMERS ARE DREAMING THEIR DREAMS
THE GOAL SETTERS ARE LIVING THEIRS.**

I dream my dreams; I create an action plan for my dreams; I pay the price for my dreams
with hard work and sacrifice; I live my dreams.

Turn your...

DREAMS

INTO

GOALS

And your...

GOALS

INTO

REALITIES

THE RULES
Setting a goal is not the main thing.
It is deciding how you will go about achieving it and staying with your plan.
-Tom Landry

There are five important rules to remember about goal setting.

A goal must be...

1. **Specific, clear and measurable.**

2. **Set to a deadline.**

3. **Broken down into achievable steps.**

4. **Written down.**

5. **Realistic or outrageous (depending on the goal.)**

I plan every workout around my goals.

RULE # 1

A GOAL

MUST BE

SPECIFIC

CLEAR

AND

MEASURABLE

RULE # 1

*I feel that the most important step in any major accomplishment
is setting a specific goal.
-Kurt Thomas*

For example:

"I WANT TO BE A GREAT GYMNAST."

This is not a goal. It is a wish. An unclear, non-specific and unmeasurable wish.

This is a goal:

"I WILL HAVE A DOUBLE BACK TUCK IN MY FLOOR ROUTINE
BY STATES, THIS SEASON."

This statement is clear and specific. It is also measurable. If there is no double back tuck in our routine on the day of the state championships then we blew this goal.

I know **exactly** what I want.

RULE # 2

A GOAL

MUST BE

SET TO A

DEADLINE

RULE # 2
You can't rely on just talent to win.
-Scott Young

A goal without a deadline has no sense of urgency. When we don't care how long it takes to achieve a goal, we may never get started on it.

For example:

Sally says...

"I will do ten Tsuks"

Oh really? Big deal! When will Sally do ten Tsuks? Next week? Next month? One a month for the next ten months? Sally may want to consider rewording her goal this way:

"I will do ten Tsuks, **today!**"

I know my abilities and I set realistic target dates for all my goals.

RULE # 3

A GOAL

MUST BE

BROKEN DOWN

INTO ACHIEVABLE

STEPS

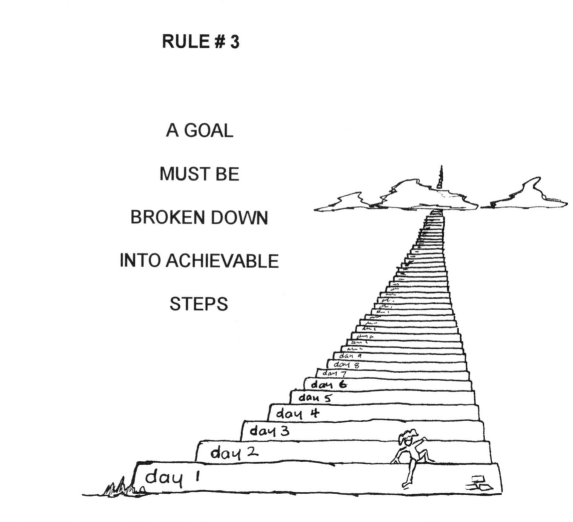

RULE # 3

Focus on the small obtainable goals that can lead to your dreams.
-Bart Conners

The key to understanding the concept of achievable steps is to always be asking yourself this question:

WHAT SMALL STEP CAN I TAKE
TOWARDS MY GOALS
RIGHT NOW?

Picture a 12 year old gymnast with the dream/goal of one day being able to perform a double back layout on floor. Would he/she be more productive crashing on poorly attempted double layouts, or, would he/she be more productive perfecting round offs, back handsprings and high single layouts?

The answer is obvious!

We must break our big goals down into achievable little pieces that we can accomplish at every workout. This not only develops our physical skills but also builds our self-confidence.

I willingly pay the price for my big dreams.
I pay one penny at a time every time I get up on the apparatus.

RULE # 4

A GOAL

MUST BE

WRITTEN DOWN

RULE # 4

Writing down your goal is the first step towards being truly committed to achieving it.
A goal without a commitment is not a goal at all; it's just a nice idea.
-M.G.

Something special happens to a goal once it is committed to paper. Somehow it becomes more real and has more impact.

Goals can be written down...

On large sheets of paper and then taped on the ceiling over your bed.

In your personal or training diary.

On those sticky little yellow note pads and then plastered all over your bedroom mirror.

Anywhere else you can think of.

And then...

READ THEM AND UPDATE THEM EVERY DAY.

I set aside a few minutes of every day to be alone
so I can reread and adjust my goals.

RULE # 5

SHORT RANGE

AND TODAY GOALS

MUST BE

REALISTIC

****

LONG RANGE GOALS

MUST BE

OUTRAGEOUS

RULE # 5

*...Keep your mind focused on your goals and off the many obstacles
that will arise when you are striving to do your best.*
-Kurt Thomas

OLYMPIC CHAMPION! Was this a very realistic goal for a young girl from a small West Virginia mining town? Sure, she was a great little tumbler but she lacked the grace and flexibility to be a top all-arounder. What may have started out as a totally unrealistic dream slowly became more and more realistic with every workout. And then, on one warm summer evening at the 1984 Olympics Mary Lou Retton's outrageous dream became a reality.

The beauty of being a dreamer and a doer is that the limits of your potential are unexplored territory. So, as for long range goals, dream big. Set goals that will inspire you whether they are realistic or not. Then, remembering rule #3, break those big goals down into achievable steps that you can do every day.

Don't forget, Mary Lou did not become an Olympic champion just by dreaming about the Olympics, she became Olympic champion by knowing what she had to do every day...and then doing it **every day.**

In ten years time I'm going to perform the world's first quad flip on floor.
But today I'm going to perfect my back handspring.

YOU CAN'T

ACHIEVE

BIG DREAMS

IF ALL YOU SET ARE

SMALL GOALS

LONG RANGE GOALS
(5 to 10 years or more)

... my father said, "why don't you plan on being the president of the Ford Motor Company someday." I mean, that's how my parents are - nothing seems too far fetched.
-Bart Conners

Long range goals are our dreams. **So dream big.** We set these goals as our desired destination. They should be outrageous and even unrealistic. We have no way of knowing what kinds of people we will be in ten years, therefore our long range goals must not be limited by our present self-image.

Also remember, as we change, so should our long range goals. As we improve and become better gymnasts, old goals may become limits once we have achieved them. If this happens we must abandon the old goals and replace them with new higher goals.

Our long range goals are one of the main reasons we do gymnastics in the first place. We must therefore set goals that will inspire us through every tough workout and moment of self-doubt.

If I shoot for the stars and fall short I'll still make it to the moon;
but if I only shoot for the moon and fall short I may not even
get off the ground.

NOTHING

IS MORE

INSPIRING

THAN A RECENT

SUCCESS

MEDIUM AND SHORT RANGE GOALS
(One year to one week)
The ones who want to achieve and win motivate themselves.
-Mike Ditka.

Medium range goals are a great way to test yourself to see if you are still on course to your long range goals. You can also use these goals to plan out a whole season of workouts. By listing the skills you will be performing in routines by the end of the season you can stay focused at every workout.

Short range goals are the key to a productive week. They can be what you plan to do at your next meet. Sometimes, long and even medium range goals can seem very distant and unreachable. Short range goals on the other hand can be set and achieved quickly. This can be a welcome shot of inspiration during those long weeks leading up to big meets.

Your training can be compared to navigating a twisting river. Most of the time it's impossible to see your eventual destination (your long range goal.) However, you can always see to the next bend (your short range goal.) Sometimes it's a good idea to forget about your long range goals for a while and instead focus on that next bend.

By setting and achieving my weekly goals I can see how fast I am progressing.

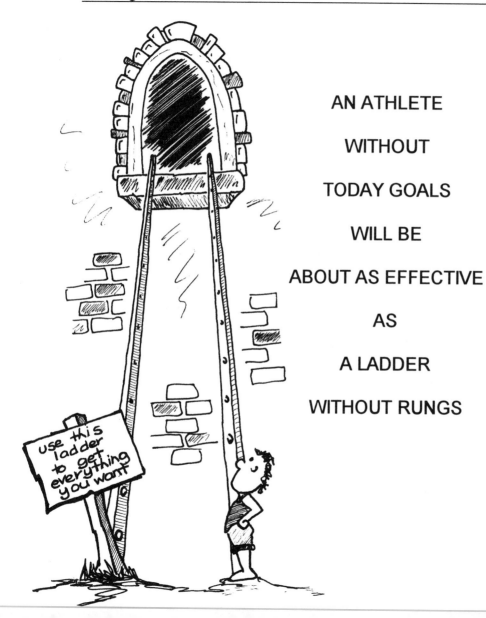

AN ATHLETE

WITHOUT

TODAY GOALS

WILL BE

ABOUT AS EFFECTIVE

AS

A LADDER

WITHOUT RUNGS

TODAY GOALS

A man has to have goals - for a day, for a lifetime.
-Ted Williams

Today goals are by far the most important goals we can set. They are the daily action steps we must take at every workout. If we fail to get into the habit of setting, writing down and achieving our daily goals, we are all but guaranteeing we will never reach our dreams.

Today goals give you a reason to get excited about every workout. If you managed to perform your first ever double tuck flyaway into the pit yesterday, then today, why not try it onto a mat in the pit? Yesterday you turned around your first Tsuk without a spot. Today, why not go for three with no spot.

You don't have to take huge leaps forward at every workout. But, you do have to keep moving forward; one small step at a time. Today goals are those millions of small steps that keep you moving in the direction of your dreams. Without today goals who knows what direction you may be heading?

My today goals make every workout an adventure.

OUTCOME GOALS

DO NOT

COME WITH

GUARANTEES

OUTCOME GOALS

*Success is a journey not a destination. The doing
is usually more important than the outcome.*
-Arthur Ashe

Outcome goals are:

THE THINGS WE WOULD LIKE TO SEE
HAPPEN TO US.

For example:

Tommy says...

"I will get a Penn State gymnastics scholarship."

Cindy says...

"I am going to win states."

Outcome goals are my dreams.

DON'T PIN

ALL YOUR HOPES

ON A GOAL

YOU HAVE

LIMITED CONTROL OVER

THE PROBLEM WITH OUTCOME GOALS

You have no control over what the other guy does.
You only have control over what you do.
-A.J. Kitt

We have very limited control over our outcome goals. For example, remember our friend Tommy who wanted that Penn State gymnastic scholarship? Well, Tommy could be the national champion and deserve a scholarship. Sadly, if Penn State has no gymnastic scholarships available the year he graduates high school then tough cookies; he's not going to Penn State on a scholarship.

And what's wrong with Cindy wanting to win states? Nothing! Winning states is a wonderful dream. It just makes a lousy goal, that's all. Think about it. Cindy may go to the state meet and have the competition of her life. However, if three other gymnasts also have the best meet of their lives and score higher than Cindy, she won't even go home with a medal. Does this make Cindy a failure? If Cindy had gone to this meet with the goal to perform better than she had ever done before she would have been a winner regardless of who beat her.

Despite our best efforts, we cannot control scholarships, scores or other competitors. Pinning your goals on things that are out of your control is a risky business. A better solution is to choose goals that we do have control over. They are known as, performance goals.

I always have far more control over my performance than the outcome

OUTCOME GOALS

ARE NOT

REALLY GOALS AT ALL

****

THEY ARE REWARDS

FOR SETTING

AND ACHIEVING

PERFORMANCE GOALS

PERFORMANCE GOALS

Everyone has the will to win, but few have the will to prepare to win.
-Bobby Knight

Performance goals are:

THE THINGS WE MUST DO
SO WE CAN GET
THE THINGS WE WANT

For example:

Tammy says...

"My optional vault in three years will be a layout Tsuk."

Sidney says...

"I will hit 15 Tsuks at today's workout."

I dream every day about my outcome goals, but I work every day on my performance goals.

FOCUS ON

YOUR

PERFORMANCE GOALS

AND YOUR DREAMS

WILL TAKE

CARE OF THEMSELVES

SETTING PERFORMANCE GOALS

The most important factor in motivating is goal setting.
You should always have goals.
-Francie Larrieu Smith

When you achieve your performance goals you can take pride in the fact that you made them happen. Of course, the flip side of this is, if you don't achieve your performance goals, you have no one to pass the blame onto. This is why some folks prefer the safe haven of outcome goals. If you fail to achieve an outcome goal, you can always blame the apparatus, judge, or competitors. If you fail to achieve a performance goal, there is only one person to blame...

GUESS WHO?

By setting performance goals instead of outcome goals, you are focusing your training around the things you have to do, instead of the things you want. This is always far more productive. Besides, if you spend your workouts focused on doing rather than wishing and dreaming you are more likely to get the things you want. Pretty cool, eh?

I am a dreamer. I am a doer.

WHAT THIS CHAPTER MEANS TO ME

My most outrageous gymnastic dream is:

The reason I want this is:

To make this outrageous dream come true, what kind of a gymnast will I have to be:
in 5 year's time...

in 2 year's time...

in 1 year's time...

In one month...

TODAY...

THE LAST WORD

Imagine if I offered you ONE MILLION DOLLARS to mow every lawn in my neighborhood in just 48 hours (37 big lawns.) Would you do it?

Of course you would. For a million bucks you would be out there at 6.00AM. and you would still be mowing way past midnight. You would skip meals, you would not bother with breaks and when your hands became blistered, you would tape them up and keep going. When your friends stopped by to take you to the pool, you would say,"No thanks" and get right back to work.

Now, accepting the fact that we could all work this hard if we wanted to, my question to you is this; why don't we?

The answer is clear.

Most of us just don't have goals big enough to motivate us. If we are going to make our most outrageous dreams come true, we must set million dollar goals every day.

BEFORE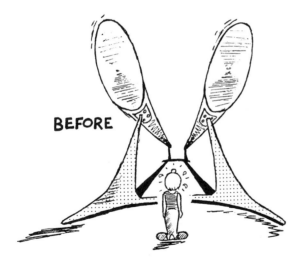

AFTER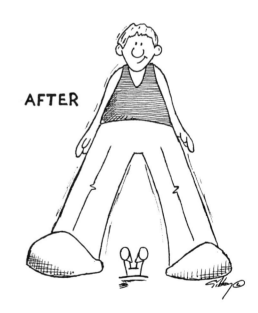

BELIEF

YOU CANNOT

MOVE ALONG

THE ROAD TO YOUR DREAMS

WITH THE BRAKE ON

****

SELF-DOUBT

IS THE

BRAKE

HOLDING THE BRAKE ON

If you think, God, I'm so scared, I know I'm going to fall,
most likely you will.
-Mary Lou Retton

I've watched this scene at least a thousand times, and I know you have too.

Suzie is standing at one end of the balance beam. Bent forward in a slight pike, her face is taught with concentration. Suzie is apparently "psyching" herself up for a back handspring.

One minute later she still has not moved a muscle. Another minute goes by; then another. After five minutes of playing statues, Suzie has psyched herself out of doing the back handspring. So, she gets off the beam, takes a short walk to the water fountain and maybe treats herself to a quick cry.

Recomposed, she tries again. Five minutes later - same result - still no back handspring, just a feeling of failure and frustration.

When I allow my failures to defeat me I become a weaker, less confident person.

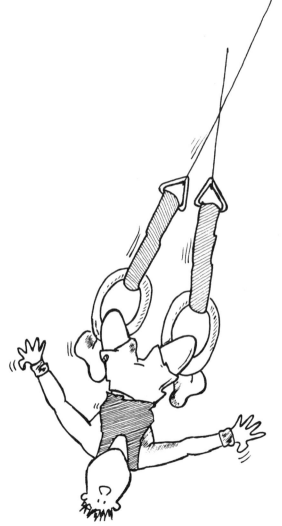

RELEASE THE

BRAKE OF

SELF-DOUBT

AND

YOUR

GYMNASTICS

WILL MOVE

INTO THE

FAST LANE

RELEASING THE BRAKE

If you can believe it the mind can achieve it.
-Ronnie Lott

Finally, two minutes before the end of beam workout Suzie draws together all her courage and "goes for it."

AND, SHE STICKS IT!

Now an odd thing happens. With just one minute of workout time remaining, she gets back up and tries it a second time. Guess what? She sticks that one too. Feeling pretty good about herself, she asks her coach if it would be OK to stay at beam five minutes longer. The coach says yes.

In the next five minutes Suzie gets more work done than she did in the previous forty-five minutes.

My question is:

HOW COME?

I do all the things necessary to develop a sincere belief in my abilities.

IF YOU BELIEVE

YOU CAN'T

YOU'RE RIGHT

YOU CAN'T

HOWEVER...

AT THE INSTANT

YOU BELIEVE

YOU CAN

YOU CAN!

THE POWER OF BELIEF

*I truly believe I can win every race I enter. Of course, in my mind I know I won't
win every one, but I believe in my heart that it is not impossible.*
-Julie Parisien

What was different about Suzie in the last five minutes of her beam workout? What was the magic ingredient that released her from fear? Why, suddenly, was the seemingly impossible back handspring so easy to perform?

Did her body change?

Did she become physically stronger or more coordinated?

Did somebody wave a magic wand?

Did her coach force her to do it?

No, no, no, and no!

**THE ONLY THING THAT CHANGED
WAS SUZIE'S BELIEF IN HERSELF**

I cannot experience the full rewards of gymnastics until I take action.
I cannot take action until I have developed a sincere belief in my abilities.

SELF-CONFIDENCE

DOES NOT COME IN

BOTTLES

****

SELF-CONFIDENCE

COMES IN

CANS

SELF-CONFIDENCE

Experience tells you what to do;
confidence allows you to do it.
-Stan Smith

A sincere feeling of belief in our abilities is essential if we are going to keep moving along the road to our dreams.

Wouldn't it be great if we could go to the local health food store and pick up a half liter bottle of self-belief and a carton of self-confidence? Unfortunately, self-belief and self-confidence do not come in bottles or in cartons. They do, however, come in cans.

CANS?

Yes, that's right, I said cans. These kinds of cans:

I can do a backward roll
I can do a back handspring
I can do a back tuck
I can do a back layout
I can do a double back tuck
I can do a double back layout

I cannot fake self-belief. Belief in myself is the result of self-confidence born,
through trying new things, and choosing to grow stronger from the experience.

"I CANS"

ARE THE

GOLD BARS

IN YOUR PERSONAL

SELF-CONFIDENCE

TREASURE CHEST

BE A "SELF- CONFIDENCE" MILLIONAIRE

A man can be as great as he wants to be.
-Vince Lombardi

Imagine if we earned a $1000 every time we learned something new. With just a 1000 "I CANS" we would all be self-confidence millionaires. COOL!

Well, that is exactly how we become rich in self-confidence.

Would you like to be a self-confidence millionaire in about three years or so? You can if you want to. All you need to do is collect as many $1000 "I CANS" as possible.

THE MORE I CANS
YOU COLLECT,
THE RICHER
YOU WILL
BECOME.

Oh, by the way, don't forget that these $1000 gold bars often come wrapped in fear or self-doubt or other nasty stuff. Rarely do they come easily. Bummer! I know! There is nothing you or I can do to change that. So why not just accept that as the price you have to pay for becoming a self-confidence millionaire, and go after them anyway?

To be rich in self-confidence is the sweetest and most rewarding wealth I will ever earn.

WHAT'S IN YOUR "I CAN" TREASURE CHEST?

1.   =$1000
2.   =$1000
3.   =$1000
4.   =$1000
5.   =$1000
6.   =$1000
7.   =$1000
8.   =$1000
9.   =$1000
10.   =$1000
11.   =$1000
12.   =$1000
13.   =$1000
14.   =$1000
15.   =$1000
16.   =$1000
17.   =$1000
18.   =$1000
19.   =$1000
20.   =$1000

TOTAL=$

COUNT YOUR WEALTH

Winners say, I know who I am, where I am coming from and where I am going.
-Denis Waitley

There is nothing wrong with occasionally reminding ourselves how clever we are. This is especially important when we are trying something new for the first time.

When you feel those butterflies in your belly, remind yourself that this is no big deal. You have been through similar situations before. You handled yourself then and you can do it again now.

Self-confidence is not the result of knowing **how** to handle a difficult or scary situation. Rather, self-confidence is knowing that you **can** handle the situation, even if at first, you don't know how.

Without confidence in yourself you will quit without even trying.
With confidence in yourself you will get on with figuring out the how.

I will not hide my self-confidence. I will reinvest it in myself at every workout.
Pride and arrogance are not the same thing; I have learned the difference.

WHAT THIS CHAPTER MEANS TO ME

Before I can take any kind of action on my goals I must first believe in my ability to accomplish my goals.
I sincerely believe I can accomplish my goals because:

I can grow more confident from both my successes and my defeats if I choose to use both as a learning experience.
From my defeats I have learned: (think of at least three examples)

From my successes I have learned: (think of at least three examples)

THE LAST WORD

Many people believed that no one could ever climb Mount Everest, until Sir Edmund Hillary and Tenzing Norgay believed they could, and did.

It was impossible for a human to run a mile in less than 4 minutes, until Roger Bannister decided to achieve the impossible.

No gymnast could ever score a perfect 10 in an Olympic competition, but Nadia Comaneci went ahead and scored a 10 anyway.

For centuries great men and women have been doing what others believed to be impossible. When someone tells you that something is impossible, what they really mean is, that it's impossible for them. And of course, with that kind of attitude they are right, it is impossible for them. However, never make the mistake of assuming that it must also be impossible for you.

You can take another person's advice and you can take their encouragement, but don't ever take their self-doubt.

CHAPTER 5

MIND

DOMINANT THOUGHTS

POSITIVE PENNY & NEGATIVE NANCY

NEGATIVE FOCUSING

POSITIVE FOCUSING

SELF TALK - I CAN'T - I COULD-I WOULD-I SHOULD - I AM

THINKING LIKE A CHAMPION

CREATIVE VISUALIZATION

MENTAL PRACTICE

IN THE COMPANY OF CHAMPIONS

Tzuk

Full-in

Double Layout

Gienger

THINK LIKE

A

WINNER

******

BE

A

WINNER

DOMINANT THOUGHTS

*Once you are physically capable of winning
a gold medal the rest is 90% mental.*
-Patti Johnson

Our minds are always working. Every second, hundreds of little thoughts flash in and out of our heads. Some thoughts are positive (I believe I can win vault this weekend.) Some thoughts are negative (I hope I don't mess up on vault this weekend.)

Of course we would like to think positive, motivating thoughts all the time wouldn't we? Is that likely to happen? Not really. Still, not to worry. Just as one drop of blue paint will not spoil a whole gallon of yellow paint, the occasional negative thought is not going to ruin months of positive thinking. What is important is how we think most of the time.

OUR DOMINANT THOUGHTS
DICTATE OUR DAILY BEHAVIOR PATTERNS.

HOW WE BEHAVE EACH DAY DICTATES OUR FUTURE
DISAPPOINTMENTS AND SUCCESSES.

I cannot always choose what happens to me. But, I can always choose
how to respond to what happens to me. Despite the ups and downs of
my daily workouts I always stay focused on my goals.

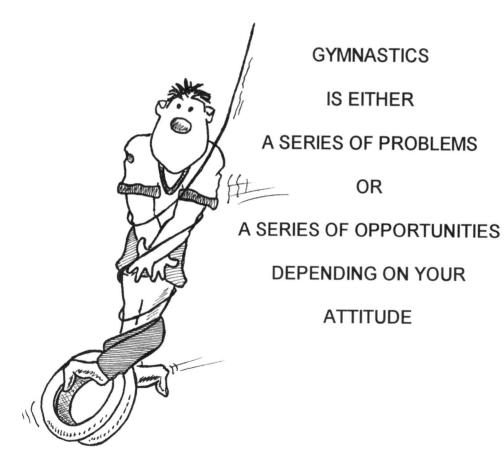

GYMNASTICS

IS EITHER

A SERIES OF PROBLEMS

OR

A SERIES OF OPPORTUNITIES

DEPENDING ON YOUR

ATTITUDE

POSITIVE PENNY & NEGATIVE NANCY

Never let what you cannot do interfere with what you can do.
-John Wooden

Most gyms have a negative Nancy and a positive Penny; does yours?

While Penny approaches new situations excited to learn new things, Nancy is always scared of the unfamiliar. Penny loves going to meets. She welcomes the opportunity to improve on her last score. Nancy, on the other hand, hates going to meets. She always worries about messing up.

Neither Penny nor Nancy is the best gymnast in their gym but Nancy is constantly embarrassed by her mistakes. Penny never worries about her mistakes. Penny has learned that mistakes are just part of the process for learning new things. She knows that it's not how many times you fail at something that counts; it's how many times you get back up and try again.

Nancy is forever making apologies for being so bad. Penny does not get upset about her daily mistakes. She knows that she is improving every day. Some days she improves a lot; other days, hardly at all. Someone once told Penny that real success is the satisfaction of setting and achieving small personal goals every day. Thus, Penny never has to compare herself to other gymnasts to feel like a winner. She feels like a winner every time she achieves a personal goal (and that is practically every day.)

We all get to choose our own view of life.
I choose to make the most of every moment granted me.

TELL YOURSELF

WHAT YOU

DO WANT

NOT

WHAT YOU

DON'T WANT

NEGATIVE FOCUSING

You always have to focus on what you want.
-Michael Jordan

Try this little exercise:

Clear your mind for a moment and then read the following statement:

DON'T THINK
OF A BRIGHT ORANGE
ELEPHANT ON THE
BALANCE BEAM.

OK, what was the first thing you thought about? My guess is that you immediately got a picture in your head of an elephant on beam. Am I correct? But why? Didn't I tell you not to do that?

The fact is we just can't help ourselves. Our minds always focus on what information is available; positive or negative. When we say to ourselves, "I had better not bend my legs," the only thing our minds are left to work with are the words 'bend" and "legs." So, guess what your mind is going to be focused on? That's right! bent legs.

I cannot think one thing and focus on another at the same time.
I control my thoughts.

YOU CANNOT

MOTIVATE YOURSELF

BY FOCUSING ON THE

OPPOSITE

OF

WHAT YOU WANT

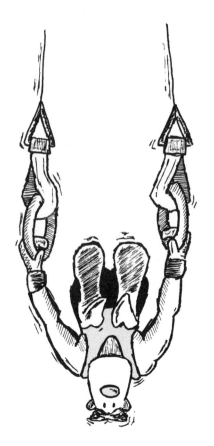

POSITIVE FOCUSING

I always thought that my greatest asset was not my
physical ability, it was my mental ability.
-Bruce Jenner

It is Sally's first ever double tuck flyaway from giants. What words and images should be running through her mind as she prepares for her turn?

"I better not stay flat on my giants.... I must remember
not to pull into the bar on release.... I hope I don't
rotate slow."

Or:

"I must complete the full tap.... I will kick for good height
and distance.... I am going to rotate fast."

The answer is pretty obvious isn't it. And yet, how many times a workout do you focus on the very thing you don't want to happen? Don't leave your mind guessing by telling it the opposite of what you want. Be specific! Tell it what you do want.

When I catch myself focusing on the negative aspect
of a situation I stop and reverse my thoughts.

I CAN'T....

IS AN INCOMPLETE SENTENCE

USED BY LOSERS

AS AN EXCUSE

TO GIVE UP

****

I CAN'T YET!

IS A COMPLETE SENTENCE

USED BY WINNERS

TO ADMIT

THAT THEY STILL HAVE

A LOT OF WORK TO DO

SELF TALK

You have to expect things of yourself before you can achieve them.
-Michael Jordan

The words we choose to express ourselves say a lot about the way we think. From the negative, "I can'ts" to the positive, "I ams" the world is full of people who believe in themselves or people who, sadly lack the self-confidence to make their dreams come true.

I CAN'T

When we say, "I can't" we are telling ourselves two things.

1. That we have not yet done the things necessary to learn what we can't yet do.
2. That we have no intention of doing the things necessary to learn whatever it is we can't do.

This is not the talk of a winner.

There is nothing a winner "can't do." A winner may choose not to do something or may be in the process of learning how to do something, but, he or she rarely uses the word "can't."

To me, the word "can't" is a reason to get to work, not a reason to give up.

I COULD....
I WOULD....
I SHOULD....

BUT...

I'M TOO LAZY

BUT...

I HAVEN'T MADE MYSELF
STRONG ENOUGH

BUT...

I DON'T WANT TO

BUT...

I'M WAITING FOR SOMEONE TO
MOTIVATE ME

BUT....BUT....BUT....BUT....BUT....BUT....BUT....BUT....BUT....BUT....BUT...

I COULD, I WOULD, I SHOULD....

There's no such thing as coulda, shoulda and woulda.
If you coulda and you shoulda you woulda.
-Pat Riley

Could, would and should are a slight improvement on can't. At least when we use these words we are recognizing that something needs to be done. We say things like, "Oh, I should work my splits" or, " I could be stronger" or, "I would take more turns." However, we rarely recognize these as half sentences and therefore we forget to complete the sentence.

The next time you catch yourself saying could, would or should, remember to finish the sentence. Simply add the word "but," and then the reason you are not doing what you could, would or should.

You can then make a decision. You can decide to get on with what needs to be done or you can choose not to do what needs to be done. Either way, you must stop using could, would and should as if they are acceptable reasons for slacking off.

I have replaced, "I could've" with "I did," or "I chose not to."
I have replaced, "I would" with "I will," or "I will not."
I have replaced "I should" with "I shall," or "I shall not."

YOU CAN

CHOOSE TO SEE YOURSELF

AS A BAD BACK TUMBLER

OR

YOU CAN

CHOOSE TO SEE YOURSELF

AS A GYMNAST

WHO IS WORKING VERY HARD

TO BECOME

A GOOD BACK TUMBLER

I AM

It's not what you are that holds you back,
it's what you think you are not.
-Denis Waitley

The "I am" labels we choose to pin on ourselves can motivate us to greatness or pull us into mediocrity. Seeing ourselves in a positive frame keeps us focused on the things we need to do to become better gymnasts. When we identify more with our weaknesses than our strengths, we become unmotivated to change.

Check out the example of these three friends:

While Maggie is telling her friends that she can't do giants, Mandy is admitting to her teammates that she should be taking more turns. Meanwhile, Mindy is enthusiastically thinking to herself, "**I am** working hard to get these giants." So, who do you think is going to have giants in her routine first?

When we choose to think in terms of all the things we are, instead of all the things we are not, we are laying a solid foundation on which to build our dreams.

I am a champion. Both in the way I workout, and the way I compete.

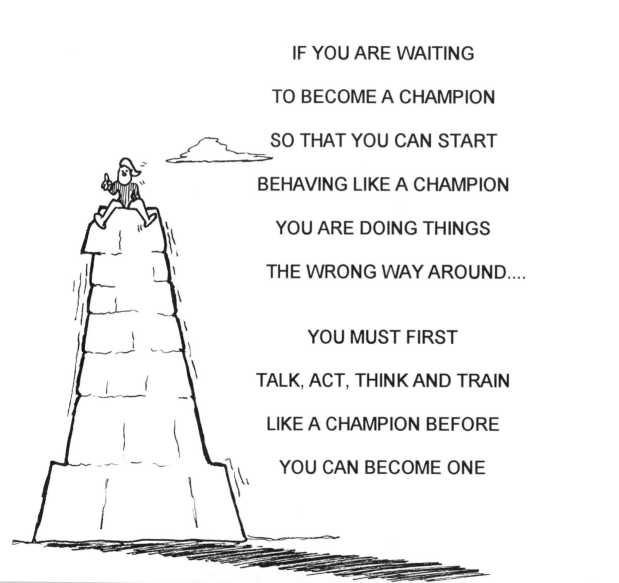

IF YOU ARE WAITING

TO BECOME A CHAMPION

SO THAT YOU CAN START

BEHAVING LIKE A CHAMPION

YOU ARE DOING THINGS

THE WRONG WAY AROUND....

YOU MUST FIRST

TALK, ACT, THINK AND TRAIN

LIKE A CHAMPION BEFORE

YOU CAN BECOME ONE

THINKING LIKE A CHAMPION

If you are a champion you have to have it in your heart.
-Chris Evert

As you are about to attempt a new skill for the first time, have you ever thought to yourself, "boy, wouldn't it be great if I could suddenly be the world champion at this?"

Well, of course, you are not likely to instantly become superman or superwoman, are you? While it may be tough to instantly change our bodies, we can instantly change our attitudes.

Simply use that wild imagination to pretend that you are the world champion. Tell yourself how strong you are and how this is no big deal. Stand tall with your chin held high and do all the things you think the world champion might do before attempting a new skill. As silly as all this may sound, it does work. Go ahead; try it.

BY THINKING LIKE A CHAMPION
IT'S VERY HARD NOT TO BEHAVE LIKE ONE

Just as a small sapling is already a tree, and a spark already a fire,
I am already the champion I wish to become.

You can use creative visualization to mentally practice:

- NEW SKILLS

- STUCK LANDINGS

- PERFECT VAULTS

- WHOLE ROUTINES

- TOUGH COMBINATIONS

- SCARY STUFF

- ANYTHING YOU DESIRE

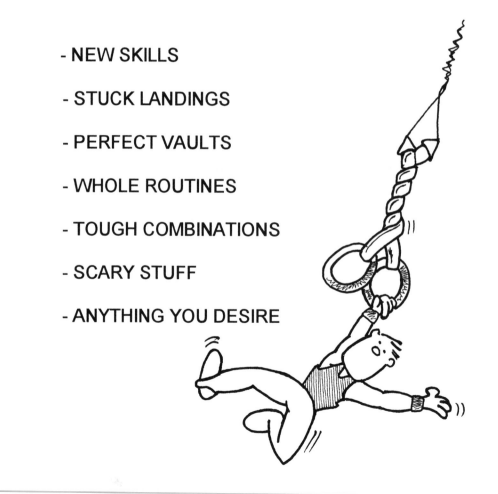

CREATIVE VISUALIZATION

Create a picture in your mind of how you want things to go...
and with that positive picture in mind, go have a lot of fun....
-Nate Zinsser

Did you ever wake from a dream that seemed so real you were actually disappointed it was just a dream? That is because, as far as your mind is concerned , it was real. Let me explain. Our minds do not care where they get their information from. Our five senses of touch, taste, smell, sight and hearing are just information gatherers for our minds.

For example, we don't really see with our eyes, we see with our brains. I will prove it to you. Close your eyes and for ten seconds or so think about Mickey Mouse. Welcome back! Did you see Mickey Mouse, even though you had you eyes closed? Of course you did. You did not need your eyes to get a clear picture of him in you mind. Your eyes are merely sight receptacles. They take in information, feed it to your brain, and then your brain turns that information into the pictures you see.

The ability to create vivid visual images in your mind of the things you want is the first step towards achieving those things.

I transport my mind to a magical world of fantasy any time I want.
I move my reality closer to that world at every workout.

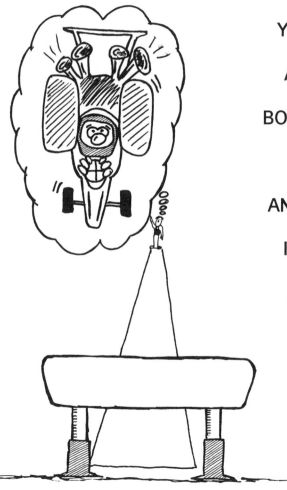

YOUR MIND

ACCEPTS

BOTH WHAT IS

REAL

AND WHAT IS

IMAGINED

AS FACT

MENTAL PRACTICE

*Athletes who improve faster than equally-prepared counterparts
simply put in more mental practice time.*
-Dan Millman

The discovery that you can make any picture in your mind that you want can change your workout and competitive performance considerably. Creative visualization can make every day in the gym more productive than you ever thought possible. Here's how.

Instead of just physically performing 15 or so vaults at your next workout, you can also imagine 10 mental vaults between the "real" ones. That's over one hundred extra vaults in the same time period. Of course, mental practice cannot replace physical practice, but it will make that physical practice far more effective.

Just as your gymnastics gets better with quality practice, so will your ability to visualize. You may find it easier to see yourself on an imaginary video screen. You may even be able to actually "feel" yourself performing the things you visualize.

I consistently practice in my mind the things my body will soon be able to perform.

JUST AS AN ARCHER

MUST BE ABLE

TO SEE

HIS TARGET

BEFORE HE CAN

HIT IT

A GYMNAST

MUST BE ABLE

TO IMAGINE

A

SKILL

BEFORE HE CAN PERFORM IT

IN THE COMPANY OF CHAMPIONS
She mentally ran through each routine, every move,
imagining everything done perfectly.
-from the book- *Mary Lou*

When you think about it, the only reason we do all those drills or watch Olympians on video tape is so that we can get an idea in our heads of what a skill should look and feel like before we have to do it ourselves. Well, that's how creative visualization works. If you can't clearly imagine a skill in your head then you are simply not ready to perform it safely. Gymnasts who just "chuck" stuff are a danger to themselves.

All top athletes use some form of creative visualization to perform at their peak. Basketball players practice mental free throws. Skiers run a course many times in their minds before attempting it in competition. Sprinters "see" themselves lunging for the finish line to win a race. And gymnasts? We stand in the corner of the floor mentally practicing the set and twist of a double full before going for the real thing.

To become one of the best I will use all the techniques of the best.

WHAT THIS CHAPTER MEANS TO ME

If you say to me, "don't bend your legs" I say to myself, "better keep my legs straight."

Change the following negative suggestions into positive self-talk.

Don't arch your giant swing   **CHANGE TO**

Don't miss your release   **CHANGE TO**

Stop bending your arms on a press **CHANGE TO**

Don't fall off like last week   **CHANGE TO**

You are a hopeless vaulter   **CHANGE TO**

You are a big chicken   **CHANGE TO**

six skills I can visualize before attempting are:
1.   2.

3.   4.

5.   6.

I can also use creative visualization to imagine a positive outcome for a scary situation (like a big meet or a whole routine.) Three situations where I will use creative visualization are:
1.

2.

3.

THE LAST WORD

One of the most noticeable things all champions have in common is self-expectancy. In other words, champions always expect to succeed long before they actually do. They just know, deep down in their hearts, that by coming to every workout and training like a champion they can achieve any dream they set their mind to.

True champions know that, no matter how tough the struggle may be, it is impossible to quit so long as your mind is alive with a dream. So, at each workout they do everything they can to stay focused on their dreams. When other people try to put them down they lift themselves back up. They follow every mistake with a correction and accept every defeat as a learning experience. They know that defeat is just life's way of saying, "It's not your turn, yet."

In the minds of true champions, the picture of success is so clear and vivid that nothing can distract them from it.

You, too, can have such a picture!

IT'S YOUR DREAM
AND YOU'RE THE CAPTAIN

SELF-RESPONSIBILITY

TRUE CHAMPIONS

DO NOT NEED TO BE PUSHED

BY THEIR COACHES

TEAMMATES

OR PARENTS

****

TRUE CHAMPIONS

PULL ALONG

THEIR COACHES

TEAMMATES

AND PARENTS

YOU ARE A HULA-HOOP!

It's not something I must do; it's something I want to do.
-James Fixx

A hula-hoop? Yep! Let me explain. You should be like a hula-hoop rolling downhill, with your support team (coaches, parents and teammates) running along side. Their job is to keep up with your momentum and gently tap you back on course if you drift toward pot holes, obstacles and cliff edges.

Are you more like a hula-hoop trying to roll uphill?

WOULD YOU
COME TO A COMPLETE STOP
WITHOUT
YOUR SUPPORT TEAM
CONSTANTLY PUSHING YOU?

We all need the occasional shove on our rare lazy days; that's normal. But if you feel the need to be pushed constantly, then it's time to take a second look at your goals. After all, if your goals are not motivating you, other people certainly will not.

Every individual success is the result of a team effort, and I am the captain of my team.

IT'S NOT

WHAT YOU'VE GOT

THAT COUNTS...

IT'S WHAT YOU

CHOOSE

TO DO WITH

WHAT YOU'VE GOT

THAT COUNTS

INNER DRIVE

Other people may not have had high expectations for me...
but I had high expectations for myself.
-Shannon Miller

The most successful gymnasts are rarely the ones with the all the talent and opportunity. More often they are the ones with the most...

DETERMINATION

Kenny has been fooling himself that great coaches, a great gym and his natural talent are all it's going to take to be a big success. Sadly, Kenny is setting himself up for a very disappointing gymnastics career. College teams are full of burned out super talents like Kenny who never discovered their full potential. Talent and opportunity only get you into the game and allow you to compete with the best. Whether or not you become one of the best will be determined by what you do with that talent and opportunity.

If you are going to discover your full potential it will happen for one reason only...

BECAUSE **YOU** ARE **DETERMINED** TO MAKE IT HAPPEN; **NO MATTER WHAT!**

I don't waste my time wishing I was more talented. I just make full use of the talent I have.

KEEP DOING

THE UNCOMFORTABLE THINGS

UNTIL THEY BECOME COMFORTABLE.

THEN LOOK AROUND FOR

NEW UNCOMFORTABLE THINGS TO DO.

COMFORT ZONES

You just have to learn to live with discomfort.
-Mary Lou Retton

We all have comfort zones surrounding us every day. Almost every action we take lays inside one. For example: Imagine it's your first time trying a giant flyaway. You are probably going to feel very uncomfortable. That's OK. Now, after you have safely completed 20 or 30 giant flyaways do you still feel uncomfortable? Hopefully not. What happened was a shift in your comfort zone.

The key to improving fast in your gymnastics is to spend as little time as possible feeling comfortable. Once you have learned a new skill there will follow a period of time when the new skill is no longer a challenge. This is your body's way of saying, "Hey! Get off your rear end buddy! This stuff is getting too easy, I need a new challenge." When this happens you need to start asking yourself, "OK, what would make me feel a little uncomfortable again?"

Sadly, some gymnasts spend almost every workout nicely protected inside their little comfort zones. They make all kinds of excuses as to why they can't work a beam series or a high bar dismount. These people are comfort addicts. They never want to try new challenges or learn new skills. They avoid hard work like it was an enemy and would never dream of taking the slightest risk.

What unbelievably boring lives these people live!

I push the edges of my comfort zones at every workout

IT'S HUMAN NATURE

TO ADOPT THE

ATTITUDES

BELIEFS,

AND WORK HABITS

OF OUR TEAMMATES

SPOT THE NEW KID ON TEAM

LIZARDS IN THE LOCKER ROOM

If you've got enough enthusiasm so it infects other people,
everybody's going to do better...
-Willie Mays

Did you ever have someone move to your area from a different part of the country? Did they speak kind of funny? Do they still speak as funny now as they did then? My guess would be they lost a little of their regional accent and probably even picked up a little of your accent. This is called the chameleon effect. Just like those weird lizards that change their skin color to match their environment we humans also change ourselves to fit into our environment.

If we hang around teammates who spend most of their workout complaining and whining we will tend to end up as complainers and whiners ourselves. If our fellow gymnasts are lazy and unmotivated we also run the risk of becoming lazy and unmotivated. This is very bad news. However, the opposite is also true. If we belong to a team of focused, goal setting, hard working winners we will probably end up just like them. This is very good news.

Look around your gym. Very carefully, choose whom you would most like to be like. Allow yourself to be influenced by this group of people only. Notice how hard they work. How many turns do they take? Do they listen to their coach? Are they self-motivated? By doing this you can make the chameleon effect work in your favor.

Lazy, unmotivated people will never distract me from my dreams.

YOUR PERSONAL SCORE

MAY NOT ALWAYS EFFECT

THE TEAM SCORE BUT...

YOUR ATTITUDE

ALWAYS WILL

ATTITUDE COUNTS

When the game is over I just want to look at myself in the mirror
-win or lose-and know that I gave it everything I had,
and that I didn't let anyone down
-Joe Montana.

Wouldn't it be great if we could hit every routine at every meet and always count towards the team score? Unfortunately that doesn't happen even to the most talented gymnasts. There are times, due to injury or a lousy routine, when we must all deal with the fact that our score is not going to count. So what is left to do? Sit on the bench and feel sorry for ourselves? No way!

True winners know that they cannot always control the outcome of every routine, but they can always control their attitude. Your score may not boost the team score but your ability to bounce back and start cheering on your teammates certainly will. Once you have allowed yourself a minute or so to feel down it's time to...

STOP
FEELING SORRY FOR YOURSELF AND
START
GETTING EXCITED FOR YOUR TEAM

There is more to being on a team than just scoring points.

WHINERS...

CAN LIST
MANY REASONS
WHY THEY
ARE NOT SUCCEEDING

****

WINNERS...

HAVE A
SIMILAR LIST
EXCEPT FOR THEM
IT'S A LIST
OF REASONS
WHY THEY HAVE TO
WORK HARDER

ARE YOU A WINNER OR A WHINER?

A winner never whines.
-Paul Brown

Do you always have a quick excuse prepared every time your coach criticizes your performance.

Wanda the whiner says:

"I can't do a split cause I'm too stiff."

Wendy the winner says:

"Because my flexibility was so poor, I came into workout a half hour early for a whole month, just to get my splits down before states."

True winners are not people without problems (everybody has problems). True winners are people who recognize their problems and work hard to fix them.

CHOOSE TO BE A PROBLEM SOLVER NOT A PROBLEM AVOIDER.

THE BEST WAY

TO ANNOUNCE

TO THE WHOLE WORLD

THAT YOU ARE

A LOSER

IS TO

WHINE

ABOUT EVERYTHING

WINNER TALK VS WHINER TALK

Achievement is difficult. It requires enormous effort.
Those who can work through the struggle are the ones
who are going to be successful.
-Jackie Joyner-Kersee

Whiners say:

THE JUDGE HAD IT IN FOR ME

Winners say:

WHAT DID I DO TO TURN THE JUDGE AGAINST ME?

Whiners say:

DO WE HAVE TO GO TO BEAM/POMMEL HORSE?

Winners say:

I NEED WORK ON MY WORST EVENT.
LET'S GO TO BEAM/POMMEL HORSE

Whiners say:

WHY DOESN'T ANYONE CHEER FOR ME?

Winners say:

WHO CAN I CHEER FOR?

Whiners say:

I'M HOPELESS

Winners say:

I'M IMPROVING

I speak the language of a winner.

Being a winner means...

GIVING UP

THE LUXURY

OF

COMPLAINING

ABOUT

THINGS YOU

CAN CONTROL

COMPLAINING

Competitors take bad breaks and use them to drive themselves
just that much harder. Quitters take bad breaks and use them as reasons to give up.
-Nancy Lopez

There are only two kinds of things in the world to complain about:

1. Things we can control

2. Things beyond our control

WINNERS NEVER COMPLAIN ABOUT THINGS THEY CAN CONTROL

Examples of things we can control are:

- Flexibility

- Strength

- Performance

Why would anyone want to waste precious workout time complaining about things they can control? Wouldn't it make far more sense to simply control them? Winners do!

I recognize the things I can control, and I control them.

Being a winner means:

GIVING UP

THE LUXURY

OF COMPLAINING

ABOUT

THINGS BEYOND

YOUR CONTROL

WINNERS NEVER COMPLAIN ABOUT THINGS BEYOND THEIR CONTROL

I succeed on my own personal motivation, dedication, and commitment...
My mind-set is: If I'm not out there training, someone else is.
-Lynn Jennings

Examples of things beyond our control are:

- The judges score

- Other competitors

- Meet rotation orders

What is the point of complaining about things we cannot control? We may not be able to control every situation, but we can control our attitude toward the situation.

If we choose to remain calm and keep our attitude positive, we can expect to perform well. On the other hand, if we choose to whine and fuss and focus on the negative aspects of a situation we can expect to perform poorly.

Remember this:

POOR PERFORMANCE IS MORE OFTEN THE RESULT OF A LOUSY ATTITUDE
THAN A LOUSY SITUATION.

I never complain about it. I deal with it.

Being a winner means...

GIVING UP

THE LUXURY

OF

BLAMING

BLAMING

A man may make mistakes but he isn't a failure until he starts blaming someone else.
-John Wooden

While Jenny is busy blaming the crummy meet apparatus for her poor warm up, Judy is busy cramming in extra turns to get used to the same crummy apparatus. Who do you think will have the better meet? Jenny, who spent the entire warm up preparing her excuses, or Judy, who spent the warm up preparing to do her best under the tough circumstances?

Ask yourself this question:

HOW MANY MEETS AND WORKOUTS HAVE I BLOWN
WHILE BLAMING JUDGES, APPARATUS, OR A SORE
SHOULDER WHEN I SHOULD OF BEEN BLAMING MY OWN
NEGATIVE ATTITUDE?

The next time you catch yourself blaming other people or circumstances for your poor performance, stop and ask yourself this question:

WHAT CAN I DO TO IMPROVE THIS SITUATION?

I blame no one and nothing for my mistakes.
The world is perfectly imperfect, and so am I.

WHAT THIS CHAPTER MEANS TO ME

The four most important members of my support team are:

1.   2.

3.   4.

These are the people who are going to help me make my gymnastics dreams come true. Their job is to offer me guidance and support. My job is to keep them motivated to help me. I do this by taking their advice and guidance and using it to improve my performance every day.

If I had a magic genie who could grant me three wishes, the three things I would change about my gymnastics are:

1.

2.

3.

Because I'm probably not going to meet a magic genie, my plan for dealing with these problems is:

THE LAST, LAST WORD

Who was Cinderella?

She was a beautiful and caring girl who lived the life of a slave while dreaming of the day her Prince Charming would come and rescue her. And, of course, with the aid of a fairy godmother, half a dozen magic mice and some fancy footwear, her dream came true. Cute story!

If sweet little Cinderella had lived in the same world as we do, the story would not have ended quite so "happily ever after." In the real world she would still be stuck in the basement complaining about her rotten life, blaming her ugly stepsisters for all her problems and every day, dreaming her empty dreams.

Cinderella, you see, was what is commonly known as a loser.

Now, here is my version of the real world Cinderella story. The first (and only) scene opens in the basement. The fairy godmother appears (played by Whoopi Goldberg). As Cinderella starts into her usual whining and complaining routine, Whoopi throws her hands in the air and yells, **"get a grip Girl!!!"** Instead of blaming her stepsisters, Whoopi tells Cinders to start taking full responsibility for her own problems. Also, no more moping around all day waiting for Prince Charming to come knocking on the door. Whoopi orders that whiny girl to get out of the basement and go looking for Prince Charming. "But what if I don't find him?" Cinderella whines. "Tough luck," replies the fairy godmother.

Cinderella learns that there are no guarantees in the real world, just opportunities. Besides, with a little self-esteem, Cinderella begins to realize that she doesn't need some hunky, rich royal to make her dreams come true. She can do that herself.

Finally as Whoopi is about to vanish... in a red Corvette (this is the real world remember) Cinderella asks, "What about my glass slippers?" Shaking her head in disbelief Whoopi replies, "The solutions to all your problems will not be found in a pair of glass slippers, girl!" Handing Cinderella a small ,flat, rectangular object, Whoopi continues,"Here is the solution to your problems."

As Whoopi thunders off into the sunset, Cinderella is left standing in the basement. She is not sitting in a golden coach, dressed in a beautiful ball gown, and there are no handsome servants ready to take her to the ball. Feeling just a little bummed out Cinderella looks down at the one thing the fairy godmother did leave her; the only thing she really needs to make all her dreams come true.

Excited by the promise that this magical gift will instantly turn her life around, Cinders flips over the object and is shocked to see her own face starring right back at her. What was the magical gift that contained all the answers to Cinderella's problems? Yep! You guessed right! A mirror.

The most important words in this whole book are on the next page. Hold on! Don't turn the page yet. Stop! Take a deep breath! Are you ready? OK, go ahead... turn the page.

DON'T BE A CINDERELLA

YOUR COACH IS NOT YOUR FAIRY GODMOTHER, YOUR PARENTS ARE NOT MAGIC MICE AND YOUR PRINCE CHARMING DREAM WILL NEVER COME LOOKING FOR YOU.

THIS IS THE REAL WORLD, AND IN THE REAL WORLD IT'S UP TO YOU TO MAKE YOUR DREAMS COME TRUE WITH CAREFUL PLANNING, HARD WORK AND DETERMINATION.

SEE YOU AT THE BALL!

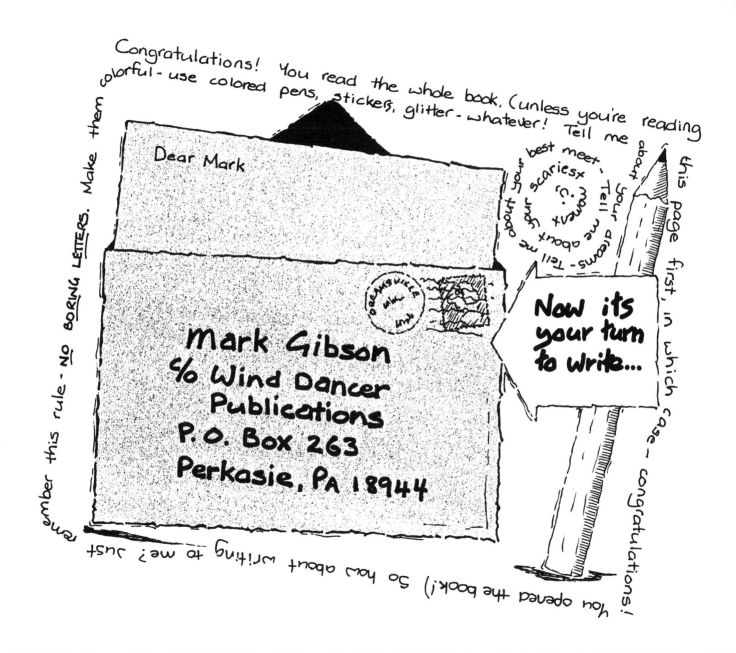

Congratulations! You read the whole book, (unless you're reading this page first, in which case - congratulations - you opened the book!) So how about writing to me? Just remember this rule - NO BORING LETTERS. Make them colorful - use colored pens, stickers, glitter - whatever! Tell me about your best meet - Tell me about your scariest moment - Tell me about your dreams - Tell me about your

Dear Mark

DREAMSVILLE USA

Mark Gibson
c/o Wind Dancer
Publications
P.O. Box 263
Perkasie, PA 18944

Now its
your turn
to write...

Use these pages to scribble down any thoughts or ideas
that pop into your head as you read this book.

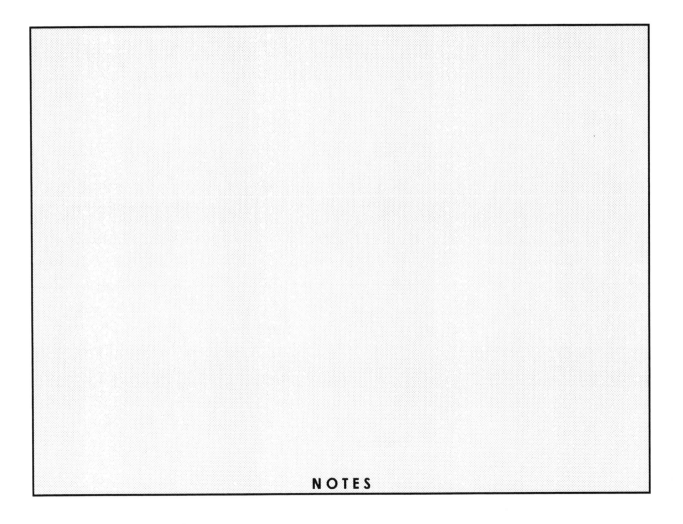

NOTES

NOTES

NOTES

NOTES

NOTES

NOTES

NOTES

NOTES